Blue Skies—Limitless Horizons

By

Miriam Green Madison

ISBN: 0-7596-7573-2

This book is printed on acid free paper.

1stBooks - rev. 03/11/02

ACKNOWLEDGMENTS

For my children, Michael and Harriet,
who never lost faith in their mom

For Lorraine and Stephen Walker,
whose editing and artistic abilities
helped in this creative effort

For James and Barbara Green,
who always encouraged me to follow my dreams

For George Foster's contribution:
About the Author/Book

For my Tattnall Square Presbyterian
Church family

TABLE OF CONTENTS

BE A MAN

"Don't cry," said the father,
"Be a man. Stand tall.
You're my little image,
and men don't fall."

"I'm not a man:
Just a little boy,
living up to your name,
like some kind of toy."

You never touched or hugged me.
You thought people would stare.
But I only wanted
for you to love and care.

Some day I'll grow up.
I don't want to be like you.
Bet you one thing.
I'll fit into my own shoe.

BLUE SKIES—LIMITLESS HORIZONS

Never say never to life
Or the trivialities of life.
Dare not to think of defeat.
Fall a thousand times,
but pick yourself up after each fall.
Never stand still in mind or body.
Believe in possibilities.
Accept the challenges.
Refuse to dictate or be dictated to.
Start over!
Climb mountains with vigor.
Rest, if you must, but don't stop.
The world will keep spinning.
You will spin with it.
Soon you will see rainbows.
It will become clear that:
The struggles of life have provided for you—
Blues skies and limitless horizons.

BUTTERFLY

You were my butterfly—so anxious to shed your cocoon;
So ready to spread your wings.
All too soon you flew away—
Without a sound—
Without a word—
You were gone.
Over the years through seasons
of plenty and sometimes need,
I still think of you.
Other butterflies whom you've encountered
say that you still fly your beautiful colors among the storms,
with wings tattered and torn.
I wonder if you will ever
fly this way again.
Perhaps destiny will pave the way.
Maybe fate will provide a time.
Fly, if you must,
you will always be my butterfly.

Stephen Walter

THE COMMON MAN

**No plaque adorns his wall.
No trumpet heralds his fame.
No parade welcomes him.
No one shouts his name.
But thank God for him.
He is the common man.**

**He will work through his life:
Raise a family and love his wife,
Pay his taxes, settle his debts,
Be a good man with no regrets.
Still, no one praises his name.
But how God loves him.
He is the common man.**

**No statue in the city square.
No street bears his name.
No one remembers him.
His face so very plain.
But on his death
the angels will plan,
As God welcomes His friend:
The beloved common man.**

COURAGE

What is courage?
asked a child at his mother's knee.
How do you get it?
Have you seen it in me?

Courage, she said to her son,
is like a race that's run.
Everybody passes you,
but you don't quit till you're done.

It's like everything you had
all taken away,
but you hold on
thinking tomorow's a new day.

Courage is sticking by a friend
through his ups and downs.
It's making him feel good
just knowing you're around.

THE END OF A DAY

Softly the evening comes to an end,
as God tucks His world away.
He bids it farewell—
until tomorrow, a new day.

His sun He has set in the west
to gently nestle and take a rest.
The great earth all silent and still
floats in the universe at will.

Silently, silently suspended in space—
How magnificent and slow the pace.
Only God in heaven so high
rules over earth, land and sky.

THE ETERNAL CHURCH

I am the church,
eternal, everlasting, unchanging.
Though persecuted, denied, misunderstood, burned
and brought to the brink of disaster,
I still stand as a light on a stormy shore,
guiding, signaling to all who listen.

I come in many shapes and forms,
but the message never changes.
I have been immortalized in songs
from continent to continent.
I have heard my praises in dialects
unknown to the human ear.
I still stand undisturbed and unfaltering.

I have heard the word as it
spoke of my dying, my trials and my tribulations.
I have suffered the agony of pain
when the world had forgotten.
I was with the children of Israel
as they journeyed out of Egypt.
I was with Martin Luther King
as he marched for freedom.

I am the church:
eternal, everlasting, unchanging.
I will be wherever you are.
I am not an edifice of bricks and cement,
stained glasses or padded pews.
I am the church in each of you:
eternal, everlasting, unchanging.

THE EXTENDED HAND

To each of us there is a purpose and a plan
that neither time nor coincidence
can obstruct.
For inside each of us is a soul
that longs to reach out—to touch.
Whether this be by a hand or, a gift,
We are our brothers' and sisters' keepers.
When we find the time to extend a hand,
God also extends His hand.
There is always an awareness that bids
us to look for ways to help each other.
Let that help be through the bonds of love.
Long after we are no more and others
take our place,
the world will remember all that we did.
Those whom we have helped
will speak of our deeds.
History will record that we cared
and extended our hand,
our time, our effort,
and our goods.
From somewhere a voice—
mighty and strong,
loving and kind,
will echo across the boundaries of time.
"Well done. Well done."

FACING THE NEW YEAR: A FAMILY PRAYER

May our family face the new year with
the blessings of God's mighty storehouse.
May we walk with honor and courage
so that our faith moves mountains.
May our love of justice and mercy
make us rise up with indignation when either is abused.
May our friends see in us the
reflection of themselves in their greatest triumph.
May we walk the highways of life
regarding all men as brothers in Christ.
May we slow down long enough to
survey and enjoy the wonders of God.
May we, as Christians, forgive
and be forgiven.
May our storehouse, once full, be empty
because we helped those in need.
May the sun shine on our faces and our neighbor's as well,
and may each of us rejoice.
May we not be afraid of living or dying,
but of the legacy we leave behind.
May the new year bring us hope
if we find ourselves without hope:
joy if we are joyless, and
peace.

A FUNNY SONG

**When I am sad
and the day is long,
I raise my voice and
sing this song:**

**Sing it
Show it
Talk about it
Grow it**

**Read it
Write it
Talk it
Recite it**

**Bank it
Spend it
Save it
Don't lend it**

GEORGIA

**The majesty of her terrain;
her hills and valleys,
her swamps and rivers,
her sunrise and sunsets
against a misty morn and a clear blue sky.
We celebrate.
Georgia! Georgia!**

**Listen to her people;
her regional dialects
of southern slang,
reflecting a melting pot of diversity.
With her voice she honors
fallen heroes of the past.
Georgia! Georgia!**

**Travel her busy highways;
her byways that connect
cities, towns and the nation.
See her truck drivers;
the deliverers of goods,
the sustainers of the lifeline.
Georgia! Georgia!**

**Though not a native,
I have come to love and appreciate
the diversity of people and places.
I have come to share a common destiny.
I have felt the growing pain;
the flexing of muscles.
I am a transplanted Georgian.**

GOING HOME

Do not be sad when I leave,
or shed sorrowful tears.
But remember how beautiful
my life has been through the years.

This journey was long traveling
through valleys, mountains and hills:
always bringing some joy
but seldom giving me tears.

I have known the dawn,
as it slowly approached the noon,
slowing down at evening;
with night coming soon.

Rejoice with songs of gladness,
for a life free of pain;
'Tis a soul going home,
to be called in His name.

GOOD-BYE, MY FRIEND

**Good-bye, my friend,
you ancient warrior of time.
Sleep lightly.
Rest well,
ancient friend of mine.
Somewhere in the vast universe
you are twinkling and shining bright.
You have joined the multitude.
Your soul has taken flight.
Shine brightly,
ancient warrior of time,
No longer will your days be lonely.
Tears you will shed no more.
Move with grace
ancient friend of mine.
Ancient warrior of time.**

I AM A CHILD

I am a child—
caught up in the world.
I experience my yesterday everyday;
sometimes without hope
and full of fear.
I look at my yesterday
and hope for a better tomorrow.
Sometimes I dare to dream for a moment,
only to have those dreams crushed.
but I still dream and hope.
I eagerly await the future, my future.
It belongs to me—only me.
I can make of it what I want.
It does not have to be
like my today or my yesterday.
I will dare to take a chance.
I will dare to dream big dreams.
I will look at my yesterday with courage and
my today with hope.
The future has no limits.
It belongs to me.

I CALL YOU TEACHER—YOU DARED TO LOVE ME

I call you friend.
I call you mentor.
I call you teacher.
You dared to believe in me
when I didn't believe in myself.
You dared to look beyond the color of my skin:
beyond the insults,
beyond the attitude,
beyond the hurts of a lifetime.

You dared to believe that I had possibilities,
a destiny, a future, a place.
You taught the class, but your message was to me.
Through your teaching, I traveled to distant places,
met the peoples of the world,
experienced smells, tastes and cultures
so different from my cloistered world,
and camc to know "mc":
Came to know
my place in the puzzle of events.

For being there when I needed you and
believing in me:
For feeding my heart and mind:
For filling my head with dreams and purpose:
I dare to call you friend.
I dare to call you mentor.
Most of all, I call you Teacher!

IN HIS IMAGE

**Let me neither bow nor bend nor sway
to mentalities thin,
but rather keep the virtues
that have sustained.
Let me not be so dulled
that I cease to be emotional
or outraged or shocked
by the inhumanities of the world.
Let me not become a piece of clay to be molded,
shaped and stilled,
but rather a living, changing soul
capable of being passionate about a cause.
Let hills and mountains not be obstacles,
but stepping stones of grace.
Let life not be calm and serene,
passing from Indian summer
in each season,
but rather let life be ever changing,
seeking and finding.
When the morning of my life gently fades
into the evening and night softly falls,
Let there be God.**

IN SEARCH OF TRUTH

**Come, said he.
Come out of the cold.
You have a journey.
Leave the city of gold.**

**Travel to the east,
while still in your youth.
Search out and find
the one they call truth.**

**Lost he has been,
afraid to show his face.
Alone he has wandered,
going from place to place.**

**Love and mercy,
his companions and friend,
were crushed by strangers,
vanishing in the wind.**

**So he took his leave,
in the days of his youth,
but has never returned,
for he never found truth.**

**Have you seen truth,
in your travels to and fro?
The world needs him.
Please let us know.**

LADY OF THE NIGHT

Be gentle, night winds,
for I am a fallen angel:
A lady of the night
seeking to entice

Though you chill my body
to the depth of my soul,
I still seek out customers
for a price of gold.

Their faces I do not see,
or remember their names.
One is like the other;
every gentleman the same.

For all who accept my favors
and enter through this door,
I become a part of their history
for ever and ever more.

Be gentle,
when my service you require;
I am a lady of the night,
at your call for hire.

THE LEGEND OF THE MAGIC PENNY

Many years ago when America was young and people struggled to make a living, there appeared an old woman who claimed to be a teacher. She offered to teach the children of the poor so that their parents could earn a living.
She was a good and loving teacher and the children learned many things. Their parents prospered.
There was something strange about this teacher.
The children noticed that she always carried a pouch around her neck.
One little boy was curious and asked the teacher about the pouch around her neck.

Not a single student had ever inquired about this pouch.
As the little boy stood in front of the teacher, the pouch began to glow and expand.
Right before his eyes the pouch turned into a golden purse filled with shiny copper pennies.
"You just asked the magic question," said the teacher.
She took the golden purse filled with magic pennies and gave one to each student.
This is what she said.
"As generations have passed down traditions and customs to children, I now pass down to you a new and lasting tradition.

Today you have received a Magic Penny.
It is yours to have.
It is yours to keep.
It will be your tradition.

You will begin today to set goals.
As each goal is reached
and dreams come true,
another penny you must add.

Do not lose the Magic Penny.
Each lost penny requires that you return to the giver and request another one.

Magic Pennies only work
when goals are accomplished.
Each victory turns new pennies
into magic ones.

When you have accomplished
the goals of a lifetime,
you must explain the tradition to another
and pass along one Magic Penny."

With these words the old teacher vanished and the children never saw her again.

It is said that once every five years, she appears and passes out her magic pennies to children.
Beware children, it is almost time for her to appear again.
If she appears, don't forget to ask her about the pouch around her neck.

LIFE MARCHES ON

We cannot go back
to who we were.
We are who we are.
Life marches on.

Love stretched to its limits,
like elastic,
loses the power to bounce back.
Life marches on.

The waterfall continues
its downward journey
never to return again to its source.
Life marches on.

The butterfly, once metamorphosed
and free of its cocoon,
never enters that stage again.
Life marches on.

The cycle of love,
once broken,
can never return to its beginning.
Life, indeed, marches on.

MIDNIGHT ON A CITY STREET

Dude at midnight
lingering on a city street.
Don’t know who you are.
Ain’t going nowhere.

The school dropout.
Nowhere else to turn.
So, you set a fire yelling
Burn, baby, burn!

Every skirt a challenge.
You ain’t got a dime.
Sweet little mama
can’t give you her time.

The night and its creatures
rocking the same old boat:
Winds blowing hard,
you ain’t even got a coat.

Shots ring out.
Bullets fly.
You don’t know
tonight you die.

Dude at midnight;
just another soul.
Traded in his silver,
but didn’t get the gold.

MISSISSIPPI CHRISTMAS

**Santa came in his suit so bright,
to a Mississippi child
on a cold and wintry might.
Down the chimney with a
Ho
Ho
Ho
to a bed of fire burning
slow
slow
slow
Good-bye, my child.
See you next year.
Put out that fire,
you all hear?**

**I'll be back
when the fire is out.
Don't you worry.
Don't you pout.**

**I feel a little chill
in my suit so red.
Think I'll go home and get in bed.**

**Mississippi Christmas
is mighty sweet.
Don't like those coals
on my feet.**

**Merry Christmas to you all.
And to you all
good night.
Good night, you all.**

MISSISSIPPI SUNRISE

The joy and beauty
all rolled into one,
Is a Mississippi morn
and a rising sun.

Get up early
from a peaceful rest.
Walk outside.
It's the time that's best.

Sit on the porch
in your rocking chair.
Prop your feet.
Ruffle your hair.

Look to the east.
Orange fills the sky.
Feel the beauty.
Don't ask why.

Slowly it rises:
this giant ball of flame.
That's a Mississippi sunrise
by any other name.

NOT ALONE

I have felt for those souls
whose lives have borne
the tide of loneliness,
the depth of pain,
the feeling of despair—
for I, too, have been there.

I have walked in darkness,
tasted the blackness,
traveled the road with no end,
cursed the universe,
stumbled in the darkness.
I have been there.

I have called Your name:
asked a thousand times why.
I have cried alone at night in silence,
but never have I doubted You.
For through it all,
You, my God, have been with me, too.

OH, FREEDOM

**Oh, Freedom,
How did we let you slip away?
You were the prize.
You were our joy.
The years of fighting.
The agony!
The pain!
The exhilaration!
You were the bride
dressed in white awaiting the consummation.
The union forged and
the fruit tasted.
Complacency!
Oh, Freedom!
How did we let you slip away?
Were not the wounds
etched and burned into our memory
deeply enough to hold on to you?
Like the evening gradually
slipping into the arms of night,
We let you slip away.
Oh, Freedom!
Oh, Freedom!**

ON MEDITATION

Do not sit and meditate under the stars
contemplating your future.
Meditation without action
produces nothing.
Let there be an urgency which
refuses to let you be silent,
still or unproductive.

A PRAYER OF THANKSGIVING

Again and again You appear:
That unseen hand
guiding our lives across
time, season, space and places.
From time-to-time,
You intervene in our paths and
direct us to new and
beautiful horizons—
some of which we never knew existed.
We have come to rely less
on ourselves and more
in Your unseen hands.
Where You lead, we
will follow.
Thank You for Your presence.
Forever, one God.

REMEMBRANCE

**The voice from the past,
long gone and weary with trials
and tribulations from backs torn by slavery,
cry out to this generation:**

**Have you forgotten the past,
the pain, the tears?
Have you forgotten the sweat
of all those years?**

**From distant lands they came
on mighty ships in chains;
Across water so deep,
without food, without sleep.**

**Have you forgotten the past,
the pain, the tears?
Have you forgotten the sweat
of all those years?**

**Freedom was bought
by your ancestors of old.
It is a story
you should have been told.**

**Have you forgotten the past,
the pain, the tears?
Have you forgotten the sweat
of all those years?**

**The freedom once gained,
now slips away.
You never cherished it
from day to day.**

THE ROAD TO FORGIVENESS

I walked along a road:
The road of forgiveness.
I passed many trees.
The tree of love held its arms open.
The tree of peace, justice and mercy,
with open branches, bid me welcome and good speed.
As I continued down the road, my heart felt the joy of
generations who had traveled this path before me.
Toward the end of my venture, I encountered
a tree which blocked my path.
Should I go to the right?
Should I go to the left?
Should I cross over the fallen tree of forgiveness?
The weight of the world vanished.
The joy of peace danced with me.
Love encircled my whole being.
Life and death came together as one.
The tree of forgiveness stood straight and tall:
No longer an obstacle to my destination.
The road to forgiveness
is the true road to
becoming a whole person in Christ.
In Christ, life, death and forgiveness are all part of God's
master plan for our lives.

SOLITUDE

**In solitude,
I walked along the beach
watching the waves dash against the shore.
The mighty ocean,
as far as the eyes could see,
cast an eerie shadow as
day kissed night,
blending them into
one body:
One soul.
The ritual
of an
eternal
partnership.**

THEY CRIED

The baby cried
for lack of food.

The mother cried
for lack of drugs.

The father cried
for lack of a job.

God cried,
for they were His children.

TORCHBEARERS

**We salute you.
We acknowledge your presence.
You are the torchbearers.
Hold your torches high,
As you light the way for generations to come.
The torch that you carry
has been passed to you by your family;
their eternal flame.
Your charge is to provide
an anchor, not a crutch that bends and
breaks with the storms of life.
The lives and times
of your ancestry must be passed on
to the future generations so that
they have a sense of their heritage.
May you grow in courage and
slay the dragons of your day.
May you give your children
the wings of knowledge and understanding.
so that they soar as eagles.
May you honor those who provided the glue
that bound you together as one.
May life continue to provide
for you challenges that test your
faith and commitment to excellence.
Finally, may you always walk
with your torch held high, lighting
the way for generations yet to come.
You are the torchbearers.**

TWO WORLDS

You have seen the world:
Tasted the mysteries of time,
walked the frozen Russian soil,
danced in Red Square,
sailed the Red and Aegean seas.
Your world.

I have planted gardens,
grown flowers in the Mississippi mud,
taught children about beauty,
sewn gowns fit for a queen and
counted stars at midnight.
My world.

We have gazed at stars,
held hands in the park,
kissed at dawn,
gotten soaked in the rain:
said good-bye.
Two worlds.

VOICES

Narrator:

From slavery to freedom
From slavery to freedom
The voices cry out to us:
"Come out of the wilderness
Come out of the wilderness."

Look around you,
see the mountains and trees.
Turn your eyes to the sky.
See the sun and moon and stars
Know that I am your God.

VOICE #1

I was with you when you were
babies in a land under bondage.
I watched you toil and die. For so
many years you cried and asked for deliverance.
I heard your pleas, I said to you,
"Come out, come of the wilderness."
But you were afraid. You replied.

VOICE #2

"We cannot come out. The wilderness has
been our home for many years. It is safe in
the wilderness. Our spirits are broken and the
load is heavy. We do not know what lies
beyond the wilderness. When we sang the songs
and prayed the prayers, we didn't know that You
would come so soon.

VOICE #3

I sent you leaders to help you on your way. I fed you. I protected you. Because of your fear, you stayed in the wilderness of despair, false pride and hopelessness. I said to you again, Come out of the wilderness. Come out of the wilderness."

VOICE #4

The leaders tried to help us and for awhile, we dreamed the dreams and looked for a brighter future. We prayed and sang the songs of hope and joy. The time came when we knew that we had to put our hope in our God. The rain came. We were about to come out of the wilderness.

NARRATOR:
So on that dark and dreary day, my children, you heard the voice of God, Who said, "Lo, I am with you to the end of the world." You also heard the voice of your ancestors who proclaimed that freedom would be your reward when you came out of the wilderness. So you came out of the wilderness on that cold and dreary day.

VOICE #5

Yes, we came out of the wilderness because we heard the voices. We wanted a better life. We wanted to be free. We wanted to shed the chains that had bound us and stolen our humanity. Yes, the fear was still there. So, with a little faith and a God who loved us, we came out of the wilderness.

NARRATOR:

**You thought that life would be easy.
You thought that life would hide the pain
until you heard the voice of God, Who said
"Lo, I am with you to the end of the world,
Lo, until the end of the age."
You are not always faithful.
You are not always thankful.
From time to time God sends you back to the wilderness and
by His love he delivers you again, even
to the end of the world,
to the end of the age.**

WE HEARD YOUR DRUMBEAT

We heard your drumbeat.
It echoed throughout the world.
Love your enemy.
Hate his deeds.
You are God's children.
You are His seed.
Yes, Martin, we heard your drumbeat.

Through highways and byways,
Marching down city streets,
Thrown in dirty jails
with dogs biting your feet,
Hosed down in summer heat:
Yes, Martin, we heard your drumbeat.

You dined with kings and queens:
addressed mighty heads of state.
You marched with city workers
striking at locked gates.
Still you preached love, not hate.
Yes, Martin, we heard your drumbeat.

WHERE ARE YOUR DREAMS?

Where are your dreams—
your mountains and peaks to climb?
Our forefathers dreamed their dreams:
ran their races,
sang their songs.
Their day has come and gone.
Where are your dreams?
Dare to step out,
grab a dream,
hold it to your heart,
write it in a book,
set its words to music,
tell your friends that
you have a dream.
Keep your dreams alive.
Make them come true.
Inspire a friend.
Keep the dreams moving.
Never let them stop.
Where are your dreams?

WHERE THE WILLOWS BEND

Come with me
where the willows bend—
like dancing ladies
with an eye for sin…

Come, sit on the bank,
while the sun hangs low.
Lay your head on my lap.
You don't have to go.

Come, kiss my ruby-red lips,
as the night grows cold.
I am yours forever,
to have and to hold.

Come, walk with me
through eternity's end:
forever my lover,
but always my friend.

Come, sit with me,
where the willows bend.
Lover.
Friend.

WINGS OF PURPOSE

We did come to this place without purpose.
We sought it out—
explored it,
gave it wings,
heart,
breadth
and purpose.
Our future stares us straight in the face,
yet we are unaware.
The melody borne in the air;
the heat of the sun,
the softly falling rain
and the universe all share the message.
We are travelers
with wings of purpose.

YOU DON'T LIVE IN MY WORLD

How can you feel what I feel?
How can you know what I know?
When the night is dark
and there's no place to go:
The bullets fly,
Another soul is dead.
The world goes on.
No one knows his name.
You don't live in my world, I do.

My girl is pregnant,
I ain't got a job.
We need some money
There's a bank to rob;
You say we ain't no good.
You say we don't care.
You say there is a God somewhere.
You don't live in my world, I do.

A BEACON OF LIGHT

I am neither the light, nor its source.
I am just a beacon
shining through the darkness.
It is my steady beam that
heals the wounded spirit
and guides strangers along the way.

THE BYSTANDER

He stood on the side
as the crowds passed by.
He stood on the side
on a hill so high.

The roads humanity traveled,
hither to and fro,
were the roads of sorrow—
but they didn't know.

Searching for tomorrow's yesterday:
A shattering of time,
gone in eternity's silence.
Oh, humanity, no peace to find.

He stood on the side
as the crowds passed by.
He stood on the side
on a hill so high.

THE CALL

To each of us He gives a call:
Stand up.
Be counted.
Be worthy.
Some may hear bells
on a warm summer night.
Others may be fishing
in the early morning light.
Some see visions
in their dreams at night,
while others hear it
in a coward's flight.
Some hear the call
in their twilight years.
What wasted lives.
God sheds tears.

CELEBRATING WOMEN

Let us celebrate women
in the name of our God.
Life hasn't been easy
on the road they've trod.

Let us celebrate women
for the races they've run,
while caring for families;
while losing their sons.

Let us celebrate women:
Their achievements through centuries known—
while toiling in fields,
while keeping their homes.

Let us celebrate women
for their strength and care:
for putting careers on hold
and helping husbands get there.

Let us celebrate women
for their articulation and speech:
for their ability to love
and their role to teach.

CHRISTIAN WOMEN

We know what it means to be a woman:
To smile on the outside
To cry on the inside
To be underestimated
To be taken for granted
To lead when others refuse
To praise and not be praised
To sacrifice and be sacrificed
To hold on to hope—
Because we know what it means to be a woman,
we will take our rightful place.
We will rise above the ceilings that keeps us low.
We will seek to understand.
We will challenge.
We will serve.
We will be one with our God.
Let the world know that we have arrived:
To bear witness to the past,
To be active in the present,
To make bold steps into the future,
To honor our Lord and Savior.
We are Christian women.

A SPECIAL CHRISTMAS

Christmas Story

There was excitement in the air
as the day of Christmas drew near.
There was excitement in the air
and feelings of good cheer.

A lonely little girl,
no more than seventy pounds,
hoped secretly in her heart
as snow fell on the ground.

A pair of blue jeans and
a bicycle of blue and white,
were her only wishes
to make Christmas just right.

There was very little money,
she had heard her parents say.
There was going to be nothing
on this, her Christmas day.

The big iron bed was covered
with quilts of green and red.
She could not sleep
remembering what had been said.

Early on Christmas morn with
footed pajamas a little torn—
She ran to the Christmas tree,
the wonderful gifts to see.

Things were in order.
The cake and candy balls
were only slightly eaten
by dear old Santa Claus.

Under the tree
so big and bare,
there were no presents.
Nothing for her was there.

No blue jeans.
No bicycle of blue and white.
Nothing on this Christmas morn
to make her Christmas just right.

Out in the streets,
voices she could hear.
Children were showing their toys,
All the things to them so dear.

In her pocket,
a few gifts to give away,
to make her family happy
on this special Christmas day.

A handkerchief for mom.
A comb for dear old dad.
A pencil for her brother.
These were the only gifts she had.

Her heart was so heavy,
this child of seventy pounds:
Nowhere to turn
as snow fell on the ground.

All day she searched,
looking here and there,
only to find the places
quite empty and bare.

Late that night
on the porch so cold,
she looked to the sky
with her arms in a fold.

She thought of God
in her own childish way.
She thought of God.
Had He forgotten her this day?

Through the tears and sorrows
and the memory of that day,
God smiled upon this little child
in His very special way.

Her gifts she gave,
unselfish and free.
'Twas all unto God
so glorious to see.

Her life He would guide
with gifts she would not know.
Her life He would guide
forever more.

Her star He placed in the heavens,
twinkling and shining bright.
It would be her guide
making all things for her just right.

Look to the heavens for her star,
twinkling and shining bright.
Remember this special Christmas
and the miracle of Christmas night.

DIFFERENT PATHS

We have traveled different roads—
you and I.
Never to converge.
I have seen you in my dreams
and heard your melodious voice,
but never felt your touch.
On the city streets of my world
and the lonely roads,
I walk alone.
I wonder if you think of me
on sun-filled days
and sleepy afternoons.
The war came within the depth of your soul.
You could not turn away,
or defy the messenger.
Sowing new money on a silver moon,
you tried to bloom and show your colors,
Like the knight in shining armor
who hides behind his wall,
your shield became tarnished.
As the outside crumbled,
so did the inside:
ultimately, the man.
We have traveled different roads—you and I.
Never to converge.

DECEPTION

The dagger that struck the heart—
That shed the blood—
That opened the wound—
was not from Christian or kin,
but from one who called you friend.

DISHPAN HANDS

How is it that no one cares,
or offers a helping hand
to the lonely little woman
with the dishpan hands?

She works and cooks all day long
for a family who sits and feeds.
She doesn't expect any reward
and no reward is received.

Not even an offer of a Kentucky fried pack,
to rest her weary feet or tired back.
A lifetime to endure, if she can.
She's just a little woman with dishpan hands.

EXQUISITE PANSIES

The summer flowers of beauty
have parted into the earth,
making the soil fertile
to await the pansies' birth.
Roles they have played
as actors on a stage,
only to die and have their beauty fade.

Before the teeth of winter
take his angry bite.
Before the snow falls
covering the earth all white:
God sends the exquisite pansy
robed in velvet shades,
as a token of His love
and the life He gave.

FRIENDS

Somehow when it rains
and thunder rips the sky,
my thoughts go back to you
and the days long gone by.

Just yesterday we were kids
holding hands and laughing loud.
We chased rainbows and
floated on marshmallow clouds.

I've often wondered if you have changed:
If your hair is speckled gray,
If you had child or family,
If we will meet again someday.

Yes, somehow when it rains,
my thoughts go back to you.
I think of our days together
when our friendship grew and grew.

FRIENDSHIP

Best Friends

For the joys we've known
and the friendship shared:
For the lonely roads traveled
and the good times we've had,
Thank you, my friend.

For a shoulder to lean on
when I had to cry:
For the shirttail you loaned,
to dry my eyes.
Thank you, my friend.

For your silence
and a listening ear,
when what I said
was never quite clear.
Thank you, my friend.

We have gone our separate ways,
but I hope to see you again.
May God be with you,
always my best friend.

GIANTS KEEP COMING

Giants will always be in your life.
Conquer one, another will appear.
Fight one battle, another comes.
One by one, the giants keep coming.

Be glad that they come.
For with each giant slain
and each fear conquered,
you gain strength.

Heroes throughout the centuries
had their giants to slay.
You are no different.
Your giants will come.

No giant can stand,
with God on your side.
Defeat them today.
Tomorrow they will come again.

IF EVER A DAY TO DREAM

If ever a day to dream,
it would be one such as today
with clouds hanging low
and raindrops softly falling:
you by my side.
A thousand days and nights
rolled into this one day with you.
I would hold you close,
whisper your name,
remember the sweetness of your smile and
the light in your eyes.
Yes, if ever there were a day to dream,
it would be one such as today.

LOVE IS

Love is yellow and red,
pink and baby blue,
purple and green.
Love is the colors we've seen.
Love is silent and deep,
mighty and pure,
everlasting and secure—
willing to endure.
Love is laughter and pain,
heartaches and shame,
joy and sorrow.
Love is here today—gone tomorrow.
Love is forgetting and remembering:
hurting in your soul.
It is sharing a lifetime,
living together and growing old.

LOVE IS SHARING

I love you and share your woes.
I share your joy and tickle your toes.
I share your colds and headaches, too.
I kissed your lips and shared your flu.

I share the horror of your wash days, too,
as you gently washed all the whites with the blues.
The color of the rainbow in a washing load.
The smell of bleach later down the road.

I shared the yard work that you seldom do
and watched the flowers cut down two by two.
The azaleas all white, pink and red,
cut by your hands and now lying dead.

I share not your neatness for clothes hung right:
my closet in shambles, no help in sight.
Your clothes so neat, and correctly placed—
Mine so tight—no extra space,

But love is sharing
both the good and bad.
Thank you for caring and
for the life we've had.

LORD, LISTEN, PLEASE

Lord, I've been talking—
talking for a long time.
I've been telling you about sin—
telling you about the sad shape
this old world is in.
Lord, listen, please.

I've been on my knees
lifting Your name up high.
There's no time to feed my neighbor,
or help a child when it cries.
Those old folks need help,
but on my knees I'm kept.
Lord, listen, please.

This old world is sad.
The church has gone astray.
People don't care about each other.
How did the world get this way?
But I keep talking, Lord.
I stay on my knees.
This world is sad.
Lord, listen, please.

THE MANGER MAKER

For years he had toiled
as was his everyday job.
He charged only a small fee—
never enough to rob.

He built his mangers well,
each very sturdy and strong.
His customers knew
he would do them no wrong.

But today was special
and he didn't know why.
Someone had told him
of a new star in the sky.

A star for a baby they said:
one day to be king.
It was not his concern.
He didn't have anything.

In a certain stable,
the manger was placed to stay.
It would await the baby Jesus
on this special Christmas Day.

The manger maker
never knew the job he'd done,
but God showered him with blessings
for the bed he made for His son.

MOTHER IS MISSING
A Mother's Day Play

Cast and Costumes

Children:
Paul
Mark
John
Cindy
Mother
Father
Grandmother

All members are dressed in pajamas or robes.

- Setting
  The play takes place in a family room on, Mother's Day. All family members have just gotten up from a good nights rest and discover that one very important member is missing.
- Scenery/Props
  One table with floral arrangement.
  One cardboard sign that reads: THEY ALL GOT THE POINT, DIDN'T THEY?
  This play can be done behind a room divider accentuated with curtains to appear as a house where the audience hears, but does not see the characters.

Paul: My, how well I slept last night. I dreamed that something dreadful had happened, but I don't know what.

John: Cindy, did I hear you yell in your sleep?

Grandma: Well, let's get ready for church.

Father; Yes, today is Mother's Day.

John: Mother's Day?

Paul: Yes, silly. It's Mother's Day.

Mark: I almost forgot…In fact, I did.

All: We all did!

Grandma: Did anyone get a card or present for mom?

All: No, we didn't. We forgot.

Father: I'll wake mom. (father yells for mom) Mom! Mom! Get up! (Father goes behind the room divider (if used) to check on her. He knocks on the bathroom door. Where can she be? Hey, kids, see if you can find your mom. (They all disappear behind the divider, if used.)

Grandmother: You don't guess she's run away, do you?

Cindy No, not mom. She wouldn't do that..or would she? You know, yesterday mom made me a dress of pure silk, but she forgot to take a pin out and it stuck me, so I yelled at her. It wasn't her fault. You know, I never did even say thank you. How awful. I am so ashamed.

Father: Now that you mentioned your problem, I just thought of something. It has been a long time since I took your mother out or complimented her on the good job she does with you kids. Last week she made a special pie for me and I just gobbled it up without a word of thanks.

Grandma: Well, I have lived with you since grandpa passed away and I haven't helped out very much. I've been too busy thinking about my problems to even notice hers. Last week she didn't feel well and I just told her that she would get over it. I am so sorry that I didn't do any more to make her feel better.

John: You know, last week I needed some new shoes and father left some money for mom to use for herself,. She took the money and bought me a pair of shoes. I don't think she ever got what she wanted.

Paul: I don't know what this fuss is about. All this talk about mom. Moms are supposed to make sacrifices and do things for us. Has anyone seen my blue socks and black shoes? I need someone to help me. Where is my medicine? I can't find my glasses and I can't see without them. Where is mom?

All (except Paul): Do we hear you calling mom?

Paul: Yes. Yes. Yes. I need mom. Mom always helps me. Where is mom?

John: What would we do without her? She really never complains and we are so awful. What can we do?

Father: I know what we can do. We can all get down on our knees and thank God that you have a wonderful mother and I have a loving wife and friend.

All: (Prayer) Thank you, dear God for our mother who is the sunshine on a cloudy day. Give her a long and happy life. Let her see us grow up and share with others the love she has shared with us, and dear God, please don't ever let her run away.

Mom: Hello, everyone!

All: Where have you been?

Mom: Oh, that's a secret. You all seem so different.

All: (with a knowing look) We are!

Children: You bet we are and we want you to know that we love you and appreciate all that you do for us. Thanks, mom. HAPPY MOTHER'S DAY WITHOUT A GIFT!

Mom: Wonderful. I love you all and you are my gifts. (Mom holds up a sign for the audience that says: THEY ALL GOT THE POINT, DIDN'T THEY?)

NO MOTHER COULD BE PROUDER OF A DAUGHTER

I am so proud of you, my daughter.
Let me list ten reasons why.
You are not a quitter.
You are compassionate.
You see all sides of issues.
You are not ashamed to ask for help when you need to.
You have high expectations of yourself and others.
You value your family and obligations.
You make do with so little without complaining.
You are beautiful inside and out.
You have an abiding faith.
You believe in yourself.
Forgive me if my pride is showing:
You are my daughter and loved very much by your mother.

THE OLD FARMER

The old plow is still.
The land is empty and barren.
The old farmer has gone.
He no longer lives there.

The cows who grazed his pasture:
The chickens in the coop,
have all departed and
live under another roof.

They said his life was long,
spanning some eighty years.
His life was filled with laughter,
some days were filled with tears.

He was true to his God:
Faithful to the end.
He went to see his Maker,
a soul now free from sin.

Rest well, old farmer,
as you grow your crops up there.
You are at last free,
living without a care.

THE OLD ROCKING CHAIR

Look at that old rocker,
rocking on the porch all alone.
You'd think that mama was there,
tho' we know she has gone.

Day and night it rocks
back and forth in the wind:
moving throughout eternity,
waiting for her to come.

At night from the distance,
a shadow of a figure you can see—
just rocking in that old chair,
looking like mama to me.

PITY THE MAN

Pity the man
who from his youth,
never shed a tear
or faced the truth.
Pity the man
who from his birth,
wasted his talent
and never found his worth.
Pity the man
who failed in life
to be the best that he could be.
Pity you, the man.

AT THE CROSSROADS

Guide us through the crossroads of life
that are ever before us.
The crossroads of broken homes,
broken marriages and
wayward children.
Shattered lives speak of our inner
turmoil and lackluster faith.
We come in Your presence asking
for a clear path.
Help us to make wise choices as
we think less of ourselves and more of others.
Where there is no light and darkness abounds,
be our light and cast away shadows.
Calm our spirits.
Guide us gently through the crossroads of life.

PRAYER OF HOPE

Father, I pray for me
and a world filled with people like me.
Give us the courage and strength to
face those days when life seems
hopeless and not worth living.
Help us to forgive those who have harmed us
and made our lives miserable and unproductive.
Give us hope when we are surrounded
by generations who have
given up and quit.
I pray for the gift of faith
that allows me, and all those like me,
to believe that all things are possible
when asked in Your name.
Renew my life,
my hope—
my courage.

PRAYER OF REPENTANCE

My Father, I come before You
repenting of sins that
I have unknowingly committed.
Traveling along life's path,
my actions and deeds may not
have reflected my Christianity:
my humanity,
my love.
Forgive me, my Lord, and
guide me to a greater awareness
so that I do not become
a habitual sinner through ignorance.

A SINNER'S PRAYER

Today, oh Lord, I pray for me.
This is a time when anger, loneliness and frustration
weigh heavily on my mind.
Life seems a hopeless maze.
I ask that You renew Your presence
in my life.
Make me mindful of Your storehouse
of blessings.
It has been those blessings that
have sustained me,
So, today, I pray for me.

PRAYER OF THANKSGIVING

For the gift of life and all living things:
For the air we breathe
For health
For joy
For peace
For pain
For grace.
We give You thanks.

For moments of reflection
For silence in a noisy world
For mercy undeserved
For challenges
For mountains to climb
For rivers to negotiate
We give You thanks.
For beauty
For children
For forest and trees
For birds
For humankind
For seen and unseen angels
For a world in search of a savior
For a savior in search of his sheep
For salvation
For eternal life
For the love of our Lord
For all that is now and forever:
One God
We give thanks.

THE PRESENCE

I have felt for those souls
whose lives have borne
the depth of pain and
the feeling of despair.
I, too, have been there.
I have walked in darkness,
tasted the blackness,
traveled the road with no end,
cursed the universe,
stumbled in the shadows.
I have been there.
I have called Your name,
asked a thousand times why,
cried alone at night in silence and
felt utter helplessness.
But never have I doubted,
For You, my God,
have been there with me.

PRIDE

A stranger came and stood beside
one certain man all filled with pride.

Gifts you have of silver and gold.
Have you seen God about your soul?

Gifts of silver and gifts of gold,
all belong to God and so does my soul.

To the poor and hungry:
To those who are not free—

I share all the gifts
God gave to me.

The pride in my heart comes not from me.
It comes from God, Who makes all things possible, you see.

THE PRODIGAL DAUGHTER

I have been the prodigal daughter far away from home,
ignoring the lessons of life that you taught me.
My inheritance I have squandered
and principles abandoned.
The transition from child to adulthood has
been difficult and challenging.
I find the world a very lonely place.
The friends who were with me when times were good,
no longer find my company a necessity
now that I have
reached the lower level of this plateau.
Mom, forgive my stupidity.
Forgive these eyes that could not see
or comprehend the depth of your love.
The old saying that the love of a mother
for her child has no strings or limits,
but like a river, goes on and on,
reminds me of how your love has been for me.
I, like the prodigal son, have turned my sight toward home
and the family I left behind.
I need the love and touch of those I love.
I deserve nothing.
I have nothing.
I ask only that you,
like the father of the prodigal son,
accept me back into your heart:
into your life.
Until we meet,
I love you.

THE RAIN

The earth, dusty and dry,
gasped for breath as it
looked to the sky.
No rain had fallen
to ease its thirsty crust.
The planted seeds lay still and silent in the dust.

The day grew dark
as clouds moved low.
The mighty sun, without tarrying, had to go.
The lightning flashed.
The thunder roared.
The dry earth waited for rain.

Down it came in torrents
on roofs and gardens fair.
Tiny seeds perked their heads in the air.
Drinking deeply this liquid from above,
the ground did smile and
thank God for His love.

REMEMBERING YESTERYEAR

The days have swiftly flown
and turned into years.
We ask ourselves, "Where did the years go:
why did they fly so swiftly?"
Many of us decided to seek
fortunes and adventure
far away from our home and school.
The irony of it is that we came back.
We always come back.
The invisible thread leading to
family and friends
draws us back.
The senses of sight, sound and smell awaken
our yesteryear memories,
which have been etched into our minds.
May we renew old memories and friendships
as we come again and again to the place of our birth:
Remembering Yesteryear.

RESPECT YOUR FEET

Lord, give me a place.
Make it big enough for me.
I want to kick my shoes off
and let my toes go free.

Make it possible
in your own God-like way,
to not have my shoes removed
by some neat-freak every day.

My shoes deserve some dignity:
a place in front of the fire.
The load they've carried
surely made them tire.

I know that company may come,
wondering why my shoes are there.
But they have been closer than a brother,
covering my feet when they were bare.

Give a little respect to your feet.
Remember the load they bear.
Have a little mercy.
Show them that you care.
Respect all of your feet.

SASSY GIRL

Sassy little girl.
You're prettier than a peach.
Pretty legs.
Pretty feet.
Sassy girl.
Sassy girl.

You have broken all the rules:
ventured beyond all dreams.
You've got a positive attitude.
No one denies your self-esteem.
Sassy girl.
Sassy girl.

The ladder of success:
Riding on your parent's dreams,
made you struggle hard.
But baby, you made the team.
Sassy girl.
Sassy girl.

Chorus: Sassy, sassy, sassy girl.
Good looking
knows what's cooking.
Sassy, sassy, good-looking girl.

THE SPOON

The old man sat
with a piece of chicken in his hand.
He searched to find a spoon.
The girl beside him
had a frown upon her face.
She was not about to help him
and lose her place.
Her place in her love book
of characters on some romantic shore.
She closed her eyes and looked toward the door.
I wish I could have told her
of this old man's plight.
I wish she had known him
when he was young and the season right.
He was dashing and tall,
quite pleasant and kind.
He would have given all that he had.
She did not know
that he was her granddad.

STRUT, BABY, STRUT

Strut, baby, strut.
Lips red as rubies.
Skin of ebony hue.
Dress molded to your body.
Nobody is as fine as you.
Strut, baby, strut.

Shake your hair round and round.
Wave your hands in the air:
for you are really something,
in this world without a care.
Strut, baby, strut.

Today your head is high,
as among your peers you stand.
Now walk across that stage
with your diploma in your hand.
Strut, baby, strut.

SUPER GRANDMOTHER

She sat on the porch
in her old rocking chair.
There was a faint smell
of lilacs in the air.
The calm wind blew
lazily across her sandal-clad feet.
She gazed at the rain-thirsty grass,
too limp and too tired to sway.
Back and forth she rocked
without much effort or speed. People passing in their autos
glanced at her as though she
were some relic from the distant past.
She rocked and said to herself, "I am where you want to be
and where you will finally get.
I'm retired.
No more of that rat race."
She continued to rock as the shadow
of the sun ebbed closer to her.
She suddenly jumped up from her thirty-minute respite.
Super mom—now ultra super
grandmother is off to her task in the world of volunteerism.
The old rocking chair
must wait until
she can squeeze
in
another
thirty-minute respite.

TAKE THE HIGH ROAD

How often you have said to me
when my spirit was low
and down was the only way to go.

"Take the high road, Mama.
Don't let it get you down.
I love to see you smile.
I hate to see you frown."

How often you have said to me
when my world was black
and all the problems were on my back.

"Take the high road, Mama.
Don't ever look back.
You'll find a miracle.
Just stay on track."

I love you, Mama.
You are like gold.
Take the high road.
Take the high road.

TAPS

For those souls
who gave a full measure
of their lives without regrets:
Play taps.

For those young souls
who never began life,
leaving family and friends:
Play taps.

For mothers and fathers
who mourn and grieve while
placing flowers on a tomb:
Play taps.

For small towns
and big cities
honoring fallen heroes:
Play taps.

For fallen Americans,
all heroes of
the red, white and blue:
Play taps.

THOUGHTS OF YOU

I thought about you today.
Through my eyes, I saw your smile.
Like a warm ray of sunshine,
it appeared without warning.
My day became brighter.

TODAY IS OURS

Today is ours
and all the days to come.
We have found each other.
Now we shall be one.

Today is ours:
a special day to share,
with friends and family
and all who truly care.

Today is ours.
A new family is born.
May we always be together,
separating life's roses from the thorns.

BUG

There was a tiny bug.
He
fell
into
a
jug.
He couldn't get out,
no
matter
how
he
tried.
He gave up.
There
he
died.

THE TRAVELER

Are you real or just
a mirage bound
neither to
time or
space?

Have you traveled through the centuries from
some distant planet to
gaze
upon
my
uncommon face?

THE VINE

God was your vine.
You were His branch,
growing in love,
peace and grace.
You were His hands.
You were His eyes.
He sustained you
with heavenly food.

Neither time nor season
plucked you from His care.
His roots were
strong and everlasting.
The vine was pleased
with your work on earth.
He says, "Come home to a
heavenly birth.
Well done."

WE ARE TEACHERS

From all walks of life we have come:
From all nations and races,
From all religions and creeds—
We are teachers.
Trust us.
Together we bring to the children of the world:
Our confidence in ourselves,
Our confidence in our ability to teach,
Our dedication to principles.
We are teachers.
Respect us.
All shall be touched by us.
None shall be turned away:
Rich or poor,
Black or white,
Strong or weak.
We are teachers.
Believe in us.

THE WARRIOR'S FINAL BATTLE

Farewell, our father.
You are home in spirit and body.
You have been a warrior
fighting the battles of life.
You fought your final battle
with grace and courage.
Now we, your children, have returned
your body to the final resting place.
Your soul flew away in the early dawn.
The place of your birth and its people
welcome your remains home.
You will take your place among our ancestors
on top of a hill.
The sun will warm the green grass
and the moon will stand watch during the night.
Your children, grandchildren and great grandchildren
will visit the burial ground of their ancestors and
thank God for their heritage.
Perhaps the wind will bring us your message:
Well done, my children.
Well done.

WHAT HAPPENS TO ANTS WHEN IT RAINS

Did you ever wonder
about the lowly ant
in his mound so deep?
Is he cold or wet or can he sleep?

Does the rain pour in,
drowning him out?
Does he flee,
taking another route?

He has compartments,
all tunneled and dug.
I think he's ok.
I'll bet he's dry and snug.

YOUR BEST HIGH

Get up, you fool.
Get off your lazy behind.
Shut your big mouth. Use your mind.
Stop playing the fool
and trying to be cool.
Life is passing you fast.
Being a fool just won't last.

Get an education.
Let it be your salvation.
Make something of your life.
Forget the animosity and strife.
You can reach the heavens,
if only you try.
Give education a chance.
Let it be your best high.

www.ingramcontent.com/pod-product-compliance
Ingram Content Group UK Ltd.
Pitfield, Milton Keynes, MK11 3LW, UK
UKHW040559210726
13854UKWH00008B/1548